Immigration Research Records:

A Family Tree Research Workbook

By Catherine Coulter

Immigration Research Records: A Family Tree Research Workbook
Copyright © 2013 Catherine Coulter
All rights reserved
ISBN-13: 978-1489563095
ISBN-10: 1489563091

Books Written By Catherine Coulter

My Family Tree Research Records

Family Group Research Records

Census Research Records

Cemetery and Funeral Home Research Records

Court House Research Records

Web Log and Web Accounts

Naturalization Research Records

Immigration Research Records

Military Research Records

My Family Tree Notebook

Internet Addresses and Accounts

Books Written by Catherine Coulter under the name of Cathy Coulter

The Man in Red

A Children's Book of Poems Goodnight and Hello

The decision to emigrate was not an easy decision to make. Our ancestor's faced many obstacles in order to do so, such as having enough money, the many steps they had to go through just to get aboard a ship and the dangers involved with emigration. There were many reasons why our ancestor's emigrated as well, several of the main reasons for doing so were political and religious freedoms, a better life, and to get away from conflicts or famine. But, for whatever the reason they chose to do so they faced many ordeals on the way and overcame them to start their new lives in their new country.

Whether they came by sail boat or steamship or entered America through Ellis Island, Castle Garden or some other port, our ancestors came here to settle into a new life and raise their families. For many, the process of emigration created records of them such as ship lists (passenger lists), Newspaper announcements /adds, and immigration records and for some, indentured servant contracts to name a few.

These records can be a good source of information on your ancestor. They can not only give the date of departure and nationality but can give family members they arrived with, occupation, and ports they departed and arrived at. The name of the ship that they arrived on may also be given.

If you have the name of the ship and dates they were on it you may very well find a picture of the ship, and description of it. The name of the company or owner of the ship may also be available. These things can lead to the history of the ship its self. The history of the ship and company can give you a picture of what life was like aboard the ship as your ancestors traveled on it. You could find out for example what supplies were required for them to bring or what they may have had aboard the ship. If an illness had occurred aboard at the time they were on it. I have found that information on the ship used by an ancestor could lead to the dates of departure as well. I found the ships list of one of my ancestors but it did not have the date of departure. In researching the ship and its company at the time he traveled on it, I was able to find the departure date and more.

There are web sites that can help you in your search for these records. Depending on the port your ancestor used you may find records there as well. Ellis Island and Castle Garden in New York, for example, each have web sites with a lot of information on immigration and you can search the sites for your ancestors. There are other places that you can visit that may be able to help you in your quest for Immigration records such as some libraries and historical societies may be of help as well. The National Archives is another good resource for immigration records. Their web site is a good place to read up on what they have available and the forms to order the records.

The worksheets in Immigration Research Records will assist you in your research for these records and gives a place for you to add a picture or a description of the ship your ancestor traveled on. You will find also a place to add any notes you may want to add.

Name of Ancestor_____ Age_____

Date of Departure_____ Port of Departure_____

Date of Arrival_____ Port of Arrival_____

Destination upon Arrival_____

Nationality_____

Occupation_____

Arrived with_____

_____

Ship's Name_____

Company/Owner of_____

Picture of Ship/Description

Notes:

Name of Ancestor_____ Age_____

Date of Departure_____ Port of Departure_____

Date of Arrival_____ Port of Arrival_____

Destination upon Arrival_____

Nationality_____

Occupation_____

Arrived with_____

_____

Ship's Name_____

Company/Owner of_____

Picture of Ship/Description

Notes:

Name of Ancestor_____ Age_____

Date of Departure_____ Port of Departure_____

Date of Arrival_____ Port of Arrival_____

Destination upon Arrival_____

Nationality_____

 Occupation_____

Arrived with_____

_____

Ship's Name_____

Company/Owner of_____

  Picture of Ship/Description

Notes:

Name of Ancestor_____ **Age**_____

Date of Departure_____ **Port of Departure**_____

Date of Arrival_____ **Port of Arrival**_____

Destination upon Arrival_____

Nationality_____

Occupation_____

Arrived with_____

_____

Ship's Name_____

Company/Owner of_____

Picture of Ship/Description

Notes:

Name of Ancestor_____ Age_____

Date of Departure_____ Port of Departure_____

Date of Arrival_____ Port of Arrival_____

Destination upon Arrival_____

Nationality_____

Occupation_____

Arrived with_____

_____

Ship's Name_____

Company/Owner of_____

Picture of Ship/Description

Notes:

Name of Ancestor_____ Age_____

Date of Departure_____ Port of Departure_____

Date of Arrival_____ Port of Arrival_____

Destination upon Arrival_____

Nationality_____

Occupation_____

Arrived with_____

_____

Ship's Name_____

Company/Owner of_____

Picture of Ship/Description

Notes:

Name of Ancestor_____ Age_____

Date of Departure_____ Port of Departure_____

Date of Arrival_____ Port of Arrival_____

Destination upon Arrival_____

Nationality_____

Occupation_____

Arrived with_____

_____

Ship's Name_____

Company/Owner of_____

Picture of Ship/Description

Notes:

Name of Ancestor_____ Age_____

Date of Departure_____ Port of Departure_____

Date of Arrival_____ Port of Arrival_____

Destination upon Arrival_____

Nationality_____

Occupation_____

Arrived with_____

_____

Ship's Name_____

Company/Owner of_____

Picture of Ship/Description

Notes:

Name of Ancestor_____ Age_____

Date of Departure_____ Port of Departure_____

Date of Arrival_____ Port of Arrival_____

Destination upon Arrival_____

Nationality_____

 Occupation_____

Arrived with_____

_____

Ship's Name_____

Company/Owner of_____

  Picture of Ship/Description

Notes:

Name of Ancestor_____ Age_____

Date of Departure_____ Port of Departure_____

Date of Arrival_____ Port of Arrival_____

Destination upon Arrival_____

Nationality_____

Occupation_____

Arrived with_____

_____

Ship's Name_____

Company/Owner of_____

Picture of Ship/Description

Notes:

Name of Ancestor_____ Age_____

Date of Departure_____ Port of Departure_____

Date of Arrival_____ Port of Arrival_____

Destination upon Arrival_____

Nationality_____

 Occupation_____

Arrived with_____

_____

Ship's Name_____

Company/Owner of_____

 Picture of Ship/Description

Notes:

Name of Ancestor_____ Age_____

Date of Departure_____ Port of Departure_____

Date of Arrival_____ Port of Arrival_____

Destination upon Arrival_____

Nationality_____

Occupation_____

Arrived with_____

_____

Ship's Name_____

Company/Owner of_____

Picture of Ship/Description

Notes:

Name of Ancestor_____ Age_____

Date of Departure_____ Port of Departure_____

Date of Arrival_____ Port of Arrival_____

Destination upon Arrival_____

Nationality_____

Occupation_____

Arrived with_____

_____

Ship's Name_____

Company/Owner of_____

Picture of Ship/Description

Notes:

Name of Ancestor_____ Age_____

Date of Departure_____ Port of Departure_____

Date of Arrival_____ Port of Arrival_____

Destination upon Arrival_____

Nationality_____

Occupation_____

Arrived with_____

_____

Ship's Name_____

Company/Owner of_____

Picture of Ship/Description

Notes:

Name of Ancestor_____ Age_____

Date of Departure_____ Port of Departure_____

Date of Arrival_____ Port of Arrival_____

Destination upon Arrival_____

Nationality_____

Occupation_____

Arrived with_____

_____

Ship's Name_____

Company/Owner of_____

Picture of Ship/Description

Notes:

Name of Ancestor_____ Age_____

Date of Departure_____ Port of Departure_____

Date of Arrival_____ Port of Arrival_____

Destination upon Arrival_____

Nationality_____

Occupation_____

Arrived with_____

_____

Ship's Name_____

Company/Owner of_____

Picture of Ship/Description

Notes:

Name of Ancestor_____ Age_____

Date of Departure_____ Port of Departure_____

Date of Arrival_____ Port of Arrival_____

Destination upon Arrival_____

Nationality_____

Occupation_____

Arrived with_____

_____

Ship's Name_____

Company/Owner of_____

Picture of Ship/Description

Notes:

Name of Ancestor_____ Age_____

Date of Departure_____ Port of Departure_____

Date of Arrival_____ Port of Arrival_____

Destination upon Arrival_____

Nationality_____

Occupation_____

Arrived with_____

_____

Ship's Name_____

Company/Owner of_____

Picture of Ship/Description

Notes:

Name of Ancestor_____ Age_____

Date of Departure_____ Port of Departure_____

Date of Arrival_____ Port of Arrival_____

Destination upon Arrival_____

Nationality_____

 Occupation_____

Arrived with_____

_____

Ship's Name_____

Company/Owner of_____

 Picture of Ship/Description

Notes:

Name of Ancestor_____ Age_____

Date of Departure_____ Port of Departure_____

Date of Arrival_____ Port of Arrival_____

Destination upon Arrival_____

Nationality_____

Occupation_____

Arrived with_____

_____

Ship's Name_____

Company/Owner of_____

Picture of Ship/Description

Notes:

Name of Ancestor_____ Age_____

Date of Departure_____ Port of Departure_____

Date of Arrival_____ Port of Arrival_____

Destination upon Arrival_____

Nationality_____

Occupation_____

Arrived with_____

_____

Ship's Name_____

Company/Owner of_____

Picture of Ship/Description

Notes:

Name of Ancestor_____ Age_____

Date of Departure_____ Port of Departure_____

Date of Arrival_____ Port of Arrival_____

Destination upon Arrival_____

Nationality_____

Occupation_____

Arrived with_____

_____

Ship's Name_____

Company/Owner of_____

Picture of Ship/Description

Notes:

Name of Ancestor_____ Age_____

Date of Departure_____ Port of Departure_____

Date of Arrival_____ Port of Arrival_____

Destination upon Arrival_____

Nationality_____

Occupation_____

Arrived with_____

_____

Ship's Name_____

Company/Owner of_____

Picture of Ship/Description

Notes:

Name of Ancestor_____ Age_____

Date of Departure_____ Port of Departure_____

Date of Arrival_____ Port of Arrival_____

Destination upon Arrival_____

Nationality_____

Occupation_____

Arrived with_____

_____

Ship's Name_____

Company/Owner of_____

Picture of Ship/Description

Notes:

Name of Ancestor_____ Age_____

Date of Departure_____ Port of Departure_____

Date of Arrival_____ Port of Arrival_____

Destination upon Arrival_____

Nationality_____

Occupation_____

Arrived with_____

_____

Ship's Name_____

Company/Owner of_____

Picture of Ship/Description

Notes:

Name of Ancestor_____ Age_____

Date of Departure_____ Port of Departure_____

Date of Arrival_____ Port of Arrival_____

Destination upon Arrival_____

Nationality_____

 Occupation_____

Arrived with_____

_____

Ship's Name_____

Company/Owner of_____

 Picture of Ship/Description

Notes:

Name of Ancestor_____ Age_____

Date of Departure_____ Port of Departure_____

Date of Arrival_____ Port of Arrival_____

Destination upon Arrival_____

Nationality_____

Occupation_____

Arrived with_____

_____

Ship's Name_____

Company/Owner of_____

Picture of Ship/Description

Notes:

Name of Ancestor_____ Age_____

Date of Departure_____ Port of Departure_____

Date of Arrival_____ Port of Arrival_____

Destination upon Arrival_____

Nationality_____

Occupation_____

Arrived with_____

_____

Ship's Name_____

Company/Owner of_____

Picture of Ship/Description

Notes: